Be Victorious While You Grow

Discipleship and Encounters in Christ

Sylvia Ciaci

Be Victorious While You Grow
Discipleship and Encounters in Christ

First Edition: 2022

ISBN: 9781524316952
ISBN eBook: 9781524328023

© of the text:
    Sylvia Ciaci

© Layout, design and production of this edition: 2022 EBL

All rights reserved. No part of this publication may be reproduced, distributed, or transmitted in any form or by any means, including photocopying, recording, or other electronic or mechanical methods, without the prior written permission of the Publisher.

To my loving daughter,
Michelle

Table of contents

1. In the Midst of the Storm 11
2. In the Midst of Spiritual Warfare 13
3. Sickness in the Christian's Life 15
4. Financial Lack and Insecurity 19
5. How Is Your Walk with God? 25
Prayer for Salvation 29

For the word of God is living and powerful, and sharper than any two-edged sword, piercing even to the division of soul and spirit, and of joints and marrow, and is a discerner of the thoughts and intents of the heart.

Hebrews 4:12

1

In the Midst of the Storm

*What happens, and what should we
do in the midst of the storm?*

Many of God's children give up in the midst of the storm and allow despondency, self-pity, fear, doubt, and unbelief to overcome them. This, my brethren, is definitely not of the Lord and will only result in our defeat.

God loves us, and because He loves us so much, He wants us to be strong. He sees us as overcomers and conquerors in Him. This is our inheritance through His only begotten Son, Jesus Christ.

Jesus is always with us in life's storms. So is the Holy Spirit, who abides in us, to comfort and guide us through all things. God's Word states that the Lord will fight for us, and we shall hold our peace (see Exod. 14:14).

The prophet Isaiah wrote:

"You have been a strength to the poor, a strength to the needy in his distress, a refuge from the storm, a shade from the heat; for the blast of the terrible ones is as a storm against the wall."

—Isaiah 25:4

You can have joy in the midst of the storm, a joy that the world cannot give, "for the joy of the Lord is your strength" (Neh. 8:10).

2

In the Midst of Spiritual Warfare

What happens in the midst of spiritual warfare?

I can tell you, brethren, there is no better way than the way of the Lord Jesus Christ. No one can comfort, defend, guide, and love us like He can. No one can be our victory in battle the way our Savior can.

During times of spiritual warfare, we do not fight against flesh and blood but against principalities and powers and other forces that are invisible to the carnal human eye (see Eph. 6:12).

Have you had experiences that were difficult to explain to others? Those who do not yet understand spiritual things cannot understand the events you describe. It is often in those times that you need Jesus the most. Apart from the salvation and forgiveness He made available through His shed blood, I believe that helping you through events like these is one of Jesus's main aims.

Only the blood of Jesus, the name of Jesus, and the Word of God can conquer Satan.

Praise God! After Jesus died, He stripped from Satan the keys to death and hell! (See Revelation 1:18). He has rendered the devil powerless in the lives of God's children.

"Do not be afraid; I am the First and the Last. I am He who lives, and was dead, and behold, I am alive forevermore. Amen. And I have the keys of Hades and of Death."

—Revelation 1:17–18

Jesus said that in Him, we have access to those keys:

"Behold, I give you the authority to trample on serpents and scorpions, and over all the power of the enemy, and nothing shall by any means hurt you."

—Luke 10:19

We are "complete in Him who is the head of all principality and power." "If God is for us, who can be against us?" "In all these things we are more than conquerors through Him who loved us." (Colossians 2:10; Romans 8:31, 37; see also Ephesians 6:10–20).

If we are His, we can always trust in our Lord. He will never fail us or break His promises. If we are obedient, His promises will be fulfilled in our lives!

3

Sickness in the Christian's Life

What is the Christian's approach concerning sickness?

We know and have learned from God's Word that all good things come from Him (see James 1:17).

Many of us believe that God afflicts us because of our sin. Sin does bring forth death, and sickness could lead to death, but the children of God are not in bondage. We sometimes suffer afflictions, and God sometimes allows it. Nevertheless, He is the God of life.

There is also one who traffics in death:

"The thief does not come except to steal, and to kill, and to destroy. I [Jesus] have come that they may have life, and that they may have it more abundantly."

—John 10:10

Jesus said, "I am the good shepherd. The good shepherd gives His life for the sheep" (John 10:11). What more can we ask for?

These verses reveal that (1) Satan steals, and (2) everything that kills or destroys (including sickness and disease) comes from him. He is our enemy!

Through it all, God loves us. In fact, He loves us so much that He promised us abundant life, which is life in all its fullness.

Often, however, the only way we can overcome certain issues is by living through experiences that increase our faith. If we let them, our difficulties will draw us closer to God. He allows such challenges for our good, our welfare, and our growth.

Life's trying times not only bring us closer to God; they also give us empathy and compassion for others so that we can do the Father's good will. God loves us tremendously, so He will allow circumstances, when and where necessary, to keep us in His will.

We also need to prepare ourselves and be in the right attitude to receive healing:

> "If you diligently heed the voice of the LORD your God and do what is right in His sight, give ear to His commandments and keep all His statutes, I will put none of the diseases on you which I have brought on the Egyptians. For I am the LORD who heals you."
>
> —EXODUS 15:26

Jesus Himself took our infirmities and sicknesses (see Matt. 8:17). We don't have to accept them! We don't have to settle for disease in any form. Jesus took care of it when He died on the cross.

> "He was wounded for our transgressions, He was bruised for our iniquities; the chastisement for our peace was upon Him, and by His stripes we are healed."
>
> —Isaiah 53:5

"So then, faith comes by hearing, and hearing by the word of God" (Rom. 10:17). Apply the Word of God to every situation in your life. Believe the Word will do what God has purposed it to do. Then watch your miracles take place!

Brethren, never blame God for your illness. Jesus is still on the throne performing miracles, the way He did while walking the earth as a man.

He has not changed! "Jesus Christ is the same yesterday, today, and forever" (Heb. 13:8).

4

Financial Lack and Insecurity

How do you handle financial hardship and uncertainty?

At some point in your life, you will experience financial lack. There will come a day when you have less than what you need.

I believe that even if you are rich, you will experience unfortunate times. Remember what John 10:10 says: Satan the thief "does not come except to steal, and to kill, and to destroy."

The thief wants to keep you poverty-stricken and financially distressed. He will attack your life and steal your possessions if you let him.

How does he do this? Often it is through unexpected or ongoing events that cause distress and shortage, such as a sudden illness, or a lawsuit that takes years to resolve.

God will not distress you. His Word will shed light on your situation and remind you of His provision. Hebrews 4:12 says that "the word of God is living and powerful, and sharper than any two-edged sword." When we believe, His Word changes us and our circumstances.

The Word also says, "People do not despise a thief if he

steals to satisfy himself when he is starving. Yet when he is found, he must restore sevenfold" (Prov. 6:30). God knew Satan would try to steal from us, but God said that we could experience sevenfold restoration of everything that was lost!

Have you ever asked, "Why does God allow these things to happen?" Again, God's purpose is to do His will and preach the gospel to all the world, through us. Some of us have never experienced lack or need, whether for a day or a season. The question is not how much we have materially, but whether we trust God.

Notice what Paul said:

> "I know how to be abased, and I know how to abound. Everywhere and in all things, I have learned both to be full and to be hungry, both to abound and to suffer need. I can do all things through Christ who strengthens me."
>
> —Philippians 4:12–13

When we are allowed to endure challenges, God can mold us into more useful vessels for His work.

Please understand this in no way suggests that God wants us to be poor. Nor should we! According to Third John 1, God wants us to "prosper in all things and be in health, just as" our souls prosper.

The Lord has promised to "supply all your need according to His riches in glory by Christ Jesus" (Phil. 4:19). He also said, "Riches and honor are with me, enduring riches and righteousness" (Prov. 8:18).

God's Word teaches us how to prosper:

> "This Book of the Law shall not depart from your mouth, but you shall meditate in it day and night, that you may observe to do according to all that is written in it. For then you will make your way prosperous, and then you will have good success."
>
> —Joshua 1:8

It is God's good purpose for us to be prosperous and successful, but we must live according to His will and walk in His promises. That means being diligent and not abusing the resources He provides.

From my experience I learned to ask God for guidance in my spending, because He controls all things in my life and can be trusted with all that He has given me. Once I submitted everything to Him, great changes happened in my walk and in my relationship with Him.

The carnal world today is centered on materialism, image, prestige, and other forms of false security. But Jesus tells us what is truly important, saying, "Therefore, if anyone is in Christ, he is a new creation; old things have passed away; behold, all things have become new" (2 Cor. 5:17).

We are no longer directed by the old man; we are new creatures in Christ whose lives depend solely upon Him.

Christ is our security.

God does not want us to be insecure or poverty-stricken but wants us to realize that our sense of security is fully invested in Him.

During my life, the Lord has provided for my entire family, meeting every need on time, just as He promised. He took my insecurity away and taught me how to trust and commit everything to Him.

He tells us, "Commit your way to the Lord, trust also in Him, and He shall bring it to pass" (Ps. 37:5). "Do not be like them. For your Father knows the things you have need of before you ask Him" (Matt. 6:8).

It is important to know what your part is where prosperity is concerned. The Lord requires your tithes and offerings.

Listen to what He says:

"Will a man rob God? Yet you have robbed Me! But you say, 'In what way have we robbed You?' In tithes and offerings. You are cursed with a curse, for you have robbed Me, even this whole nation. Bring all the tithes into the storehouse, that there may be food in My house, and try Me now in this," says the Lord of hosts, "If I will not open for you the windows of heaven and pour out for you such blessing that there will not be room enough to receive it."

—Malachi 3:8–10

If Jesus is your Lord and Savior, you have authority over Satan. This is by God's power invested in you. Command the enemy to leave and take his hands off your finances, in Jesus's name. Ask the Lord to send ministering angels to go forth in battle for you, according to Hebrews 1:13–14, which says:

To which of the angels has He ever said: "Sit at My right hand, till I make Your enemies Your footstool"? Are they not all ministering spirits sent forth to minister for those who will inherit salvation?

Trust in God's promises and obey His commands. When you do, financial lack and insecurity must go!

5

How Is Your Walk with God?

Today might be your last day alive on this planet.

How is your relationship with God? Have you received Jesus as your personal Lord and Savior, your friend, mediator, intercessor, and most precious gift in life? (See "Prayer for Salvation" at the end of this booklet.) If He is your Savior, do you appreciate what He has done for you?

We need to examine ourselves thoroughly and ask the following important questions:

- Have I accepted Jesus and the Holy Spirit as great gifts from God?
- Am I obedient to the voice of the Lord?
- Is my daily walk based on God's Word?
- Am I growing in the Lord or stagnating?
- Do I enjoy being a child of God, or am I struggling in my walk with Him?

The answers to these questions are based on your individual relationship with the Lord through Jesus Christ. Some have only accepted Him as their source of convenience and have no relationship with Him beyond what He can do for them. When trials come, they return to their own vomit, as pigs do (see Prov. 26:11). If you think you might fit into this category, please pray sincerely, repent, and seek the Lord's guidance in your life.

Before you can enjoy the beauty of serving the Lord and receiving the spiritual and material blessings He has for you, you must submit your life and all that you possess to Him.

Jesus Christ has purchased the sinner with His blood. When we accept His sacrifice, we are no more our own, and neither are we the world's.

If you belong to the Lord but are striving to live like the world, you will struggle. You cannot have the Lord and the world at the same time. "You cannot serve God and mammon" (or money) together.

> "If you were of the world, the world would love its own. Yet because you are not of the world, but I chose you out of the world, therefore the world hates you."
>
> —John 15:19

Ask God for His guidance and direction in all things. He is always there and willing to forgive you when you repent.

"Do you not know that you are the temple of God and that the Spirit of God dwells in you? If anyone defiles the temple of God, God will destroy him. For the temple of God is holy, which temple you are" (1 Cor. 3:16–17).

Keep your temple clean and pure!

Are you doing what God has commanded you to do? Or are you afraid of what the world might say? Is Christ a "stone of stumbling and a rock of offense" to you? Do you "stumble, being disobedient to the word, to which [you] also were appointed"? (1 Pet. 2:8).

> "If you are willing and obedient, you shall eat the good of the land; but if you refuse and rebel, you shall be devoured by the sword"; for the mouth of the LORD has spoken."
>
> —ISAIAH 1:19–20

Obedience is a key ingredient for the blessed life. Disobedience, however, will produce many negative consequences. Read the Book of Jonah to see this dynamic in action. When Jonah disobeyed God, he found himself in the belly of a whale.

The Word of God is an essential part of our daily walk. While He was here on the earth, Jesus never did anything that was outside of God's will (or not in keeping with God's Word). He was our perfect example. Therefore, we also ought to apply the Word to our lives in everything and every circumstance.

The Lord never instructs us to do anything contrary to His Word. All His requirements are based on His Word: The Word of God is powerful and represents God Himself.

As it is written: "In the beginning was the Word, and the Word was with God, and the Word was God" (John 1:1). "His [Jesus's] name is called The Word of God" (Rev. 19:13).

When the Holy Spirit enlightened my understanding through these verses, my attitude toward the Word of God changed. I realized that there is a miraculous and tremendous power in applying the Word in our lives. I began to see life, truth, and faith working in and through the Word.

The Father, Son, and Holy Spirit (the Comforter who lives in us) are three Persons but one God, who works in us through His Word.

Finally, brethren, saturate yourself with the Word of God. Walk always in the Spirit who indwells you. "Be still and know" that He is God (Ps. 46:10).

Prayer for Salvation

If you have not yet given your life to Jesus Christ or have doubts about your relationship with the Lord, pray this prayer:

Heavenly Father, I come before You in the precious and powerful name of Jesus Christ. I repent of all my sins, and I ask You to come into my life. I ask forgiveness for my sins and I believe that from this moment on, I am set free from bondage and have eternal life in Jesus's name. Amen.

www.ingramcontent.com/pod-product-compliance
Lightning Source LLC
Chambersburg PA
CBHW021639080526
44584CB00015BA/1608